THE BOOK OF
60 HAND-LETTERED ALPHABET

A GUIDE TO BETTER LETTERING FOR ARTISTS
AND DESIGNERS OF SIGNS, SHOWCARDS, DISPLAYS, EXHIBITS
AND ADVERTISING LAYOUTS, BY J. I. BIEGELEISEN

Published by
Signs of the Times Publishing Co.
Cincinnati, Ohio, U.S.A.

International Standard Book Number 0-911380-40-X

INDEX

INDEX

INDEX

INTRODUCTION

The collection of display face alphabets in this book represents a compilation of the highly successful series of hand-lettered alphabets which have appeared monthly in the SIGNS of the Times magazine. If you have been a steady reader of the magazine and were prudent enough to save tear sheets of each alphabet as it made its appearance in the pges of the magazine, then you would not need this book—but then how many of us are that prudent and possess the foresight to collect and collate source material with such consistency? But even if you are one of those rare individuals who claim that distinction, you'll find this book especially valuable because many alphabets have been enlarged in format—the easier to analyze and follow—and all are printed on book stock of superior quality. What's more, the lettering styles here are arranged in alphabetical order, easy to identify and locate when needed.

The alphabets shown here are for the most part simplified versions of standard type faces rendered with brush, pen and other instruments, as the case may be. You'll find new eccentric, non-practical styles here, since all were designed and rendered for use by lettering artists in the field of sign and showcard writing, poster design, display and exhibit builders, as well as those who prepare art for screen printing reproduction. If you identify yourself with one or more in this general category, then the book is for you. It will not only serve as a repertoire of useful display face alphabets, but will no doubt help to inspire you to venture forth in designing alphabets completely your own, suited to your special talents and requirements.

At this time, I would like to acknowledge with sincere gratitude the assistance I have received from my professional colleague, Morris Kelvin, in rendering a number of hand-lettered alphabets which appear in this book. I also wish to publicly thank my wife Esther who so ably and conscientiously worked with me editorially as well as in the chores involved in the preparation of mechanicals.

J. I. Biegeleisen

ABCDE

FGHIJK

LMNOP

QRSTU

VWXYZ

1234567890

AFRIQUE

Designers of today's lettering styles are not averse to departing (often radically) from traditional construction of letter forms, with typographic impunity which tends to shock old-timers in the field. Hand lettering, type faces and the myriads of photo-lettering alphabets available today follow the trend set by the fine art and design field in creating new and highly personalized effects which reflect our changing life style. Afrique follows this general trend. The somewhat unorthodox construction of the letter forms with their heavy crossbars such as in the A and the H; the two heavy diagonal strokes of the M, and so forth, depart radically from traditional letter construction. The alphabet style also reflects a rediscovered interest in African culture as evidenced by contemporary art shows in galleries and museums. Afrique is by no means limited to "jungle-habitat" wildlife advertising and the like. The style is quite appropriate for any kind of advertising assignment where a distinctive, highly individual quality is to be achieved.

ABCDEF
GHIJKL
MNOPQ
RSTUV
WXYZ
1234567890

ART BOLD ITALIC

Art Bold Italic derives its force from the solid block-like components which comprise the fundamental strokes of the letters. In addition, the absence of hairlines or any other binding elements between the strokes gives this style a stencil-like character which demands attention on any piece of copy. Naturally the best effect is achieved by reserving this alphabet for headlines only. As such it is an excellent choice for posters and displays dealing with travel, advertisements dealing with men's wear, cosmetics, art exhibitions, etc. The absence of serifs and thin elements makes it an ideal alphabet for screen printing as well. Either direct or reverse, it will reproduce beautifully regardless of size or printing source. Try your hand in rendering this alphabet; freehand technique for casual work and ruling pen for work intended for reproduction.

ABCDE
FGHIJK
LMNOP
QRSTU
VWXYZ
1234567890

BALLOON

If it's a fast lettering style you're looking for,
this alphabet (modelled after a standard
type face) will come in handy. It's intended
as a "single stroke" alphabet, to be rendered
with a fully charged brush, of a size suited
to the height and weight of the letter. It may
be upright as shown here, or slanted somewhat, to give the illusion of italics. This is an
excellent lettering style for paper signs,
showcards, and wherever an informal, speedy
effect is desired. The chances are that you'll
develop your own modification of Balloon,
as you inject in it your own "personal touch"
as time goes along.

ABCD
EFGHI
JKLM
NOPQ
RSTUV
WXYZ
1234567890

BAROQUE

Old World elegance and grandeur are expressed in the ornate alphabet, Baroque. Essentially a thick and thin Roman letter structure, the style is embellished by the splayed serifs and the center ornamentation device appended to most of the letters. Further embellishments are possible through ornamentation within the body of the letter itself in the form of diamond-shaped devices, ovals, circles, or other geometric shapes. The extent of the ornamentation will depend on the occasion; and, of course, on the time one can allot to the job on hand. Baroque is an appropriate choice for captions dealing with some celebrated event, jubilees, anniversaries, and so on. More commercially it can be used for advertising furs, jewelry, silverware, fancy menu covers, bookjackets for historic titles, and other occasions which have a flavor of the "good old times." It is advisable in rendering Baroque, to complete the lettering with the serifs, and then add the ornamental device in the center or other decorative elements within the letter itself.

ABCDE
FGHIJK
LMNOP
QRSTU
VWXYZ
1234567890

BEL AIRE BOLD ITALIC

A high contrast between thick and thin strokes
lends a stencil-like effect to this original
alphabet. Bel Aire Bold Italic can be rendered
in several ways: with a wide steel "brush pen,"
a flat well chiselled (short hair) lettering
brush, a sign writer's quill, or a broad-nibbed
magic marker. Modification in the structure
will be the natural outgrowth of the
particular tool selected. If you are preparing
copy for screen printing reproduction, the
film cutter will bless you because the work
can be cut quickly, freehand and it is devoid
of time-consuming serifs and curlicues.
With the exception of the finishing-off whispy
lines which serve as terminals in the basic
stroke, the work can progress with dispatch.
Whether hand-lettered for showcards,
posters, signs, or work for reproduction, this
italic alphabet style has much to recommend.

ABCDEF
GHIJKL
MNOPQ
RSTUV
WXYZ

BIJOU

The black-face alphabet, Bijou, belongs in the stencil-type face category. Not any connecting ties unite the components of Bijou's various letterform elements. Geometrical in format, the style conveys a theatrical feeling on a highly sophisticated level. Practical applications, one can readily observe, are limited necessarily to headlines and titles rather than to massive body copy for the sake of legibility. Bijou can add a note of typographic elegance, however, to the following three kinds of layout. Wherever legibility is not a primary factor; where time permits rendering meticulous letter reproduction; and where the unusual style of Bijou lettering just happens to suit the copy beautifully. When Bijou is designed for reproduction by either screen printing or another graphic art medium, remember especially that the thin sliver-like spaces that separate the main elements may close up within each letter design if the size reduction is extensive. Bijou's letters must be kept as large as practical in the original artwork for the best results if the final version is to be reduced extensively in size.

ABCDE
FGHIJK
LMNOP
QRSTU
VWXYZ
1234567890

BROADWAY

This is a modified version of a standard type
face which has been around for years,
dropped into decline, and has now come
back stronger than ever. The chief characteristics of the alphabet are: very high
contrast between thick and thin elements; the
slight, almost indiscernible curve in the basic
upright stroke; the one-thickness elements
of the thin auxiliary strokes in the B, D, G, K, O,
etc., which break tradition and do not take
on the full weight of the primary strokes.
With a little practice, this alphabet can be
rendered rapidly and entirely freehand.
The thickness of the heavy strokes calls for
a build up technique; the thin elements are
done single stroke with light pressure of the
brush. If a decorative motif is desired, there's
enough space within the heavy strokes for
some original doodads (such as suggested in
the letter A) to suit the occasion. It makes
this alphabet, an "alphabet for all seasons."

ABCDEFG
HIJKLM
NOPQRS
TUVW
XYZ
1234567890

CARDCRAFT

Cardcraft is a basic letter form and is equally compatible with the brush or pen. The style is appropriate for showcards, charts and graphs, price tickets, window streamers, banners, and wherever legibility and speed of execution are of primary importance. The rounded endings suggest the use of a flooded brush with no or very little time used in paletting. For pen work, a lettering pen's "B" series (or equivalent) is recommended. Cardcraft can be produced in Roman (upright format) as shown here, or in italics. Either way Cardcraft is a one-stroke alphabet with even pressure applied to the lettering tool employed. Because of peerless legibility, it's fine for massive copy as well as "one-liners" or headlines. Cardcraft becomes especially effective if a more ornate alphabet (one of the many in your inventory of display faces) is employed as a foil and contrasting attention-getter. This simple one-stroke alphabet—or a modification of it—is considered one of the most practical lettering styles for the practitioner in the art of hand lettering.

ABCDEF
GHIJKLM
NOPQRST
UVWXYZ
1234567890

CARDINAL GOTHIC

Cardinal Gothic can be rendered with brush or pen, depending upon practical circumstances and the degree of finish desired. As a pen letter, speed can be achieved with a B series Speedball pen (or its equivalent) but the endings of each stroke will be round rather than square. This is of no great importance—as long as consistency is achieved. For brush work, especially for single stroke rendition, a flooded brush will yield fast results. If desired, endings can be squared off with opaque white, when preparing work for reproduction. In general, this style is basically one suited for advertising dealing with fine furniture, silverware, furs, cosmetics, women's wear and other work where delicacy, refinement, and hauteur are to be conveyed.

ABCDEFG
HIJKLMN
OPQRSTU
VWXYZ
!?$():
1234567890

CAROLUS

Carolus is a hand-lettered version of a type
face of the same name. Strongly calligraphic
in appearance, Carolus is best rendered with
a broad nibbed pen or brush, whether
intended for informal showcards or a
more finished style for bookjackets,
movie and television title cards, greeting
cards, travel posters, and letterheads. This
alphabet also lends itself as an alternate style
to Old English for lettering diplomas, certificates, and proclamations. Where time and
circumstance warrant it, it can be further
embellished by a drop shadow rendered in
soft tone with water colors. Carolus is a style
you'll enjoy working with, and with practice
you will most likely depart from the basic
specimen illustrated here. Imperceptibly, but
surely, our own individuality will emerge by
your choice of tool and the manner in which
you use that tool.

ABCDEF
GHIJKLM
NOPQRST
UVWXYZ
abcdefghijklm
nopqrstuvwxyz

Casual

Basically Casual is a modified form of informal handwriting. The capital letters are generally characterized by free-flowing flourishes produced with a lightweight pen or flooded brush. If a brush is used it may be the chisel edge lettering kind or a pointed watercolor brush. The lower case is a bit more formal and disciplined. There are connecting links between letters in the formation of words. The alphabet may be used all in caps as for example in headlines and feature copy, or it may be used in combination, upper and lower case. Since this is a hand lettering style and essentially reflects one's personal handwriting, infinite variations are possible—in the formation of the letter structure, in width of stroke, the slant and the formation of flourishes. Casual is a style you will enjoy rendering, and with experience you will acquire not only a personal style, but speed and the "light touch" as well.

ABCDEF
GHIJKLM
NOPQRST
UVWXYZ
1234567890

CENTURY ITALICS

You're sure to find Century Italics one of the most practical italic alphabets in your repertoire. It is practical because it fits in well with most any advertising or showcard needs. Based on a standard printer's type face called Century Schoolbook, this alphabet can be produced with relative speed with either brush or pen. It can be rendered either as a single stroke letter by varying the pressure on the lettering tool, or as a more carefully built up structure with one stroke for the thin elements and two strokes for the heavy elements and serifs. You'll note that the numbers are not lined up—for example, the 3, 4, 5, 7, and 9 are below the line, while the 6 and 8 reach over the line. That is optional. You can modify this, as you wish. In fact, in the actual printer's type face, there are two distinct versions to the numbers; one with numbers all aligned, the other called "oldstyle" where the numbers appear as they are shown here. You are equally at liberty to make any other modifications in the letters themselves—and the chances are that you will—as you gain the freedom, yet retain the spirit of this classic alphabet.

ABCD
EFGHI
JKLM
NOPQ
RSTUV
WXYZ

CONCERTA

A calligraphic alphabet, lettered here with a No. 8 lettering brush, lends itself admirably to other lettering tools, such as broad one-stroke nibbed "steel brush" pens or felt markers. Any form of calligraphic lettering is appropriate not only for diplomas and certificates and general engrossing, but for commercial purposes as well. Use it for posters and signs dealing with religious themes, musical and varied cultural events, Christmas, Easter, and other holidays. It should be understood that calligraphic lettering is a very personal mode of graphic self-expression. The lettering defies standardization or adherence to a "model" alphabet. Experiment! Use whatever lettering tool is best for you and see what variations of the Concerta alphabet you can devise. Next time a showcard or poster order comes into your shop where a calligraphic alphabet would seem appropriate, make use of the results of your own experimentation, either for the entire wording or for a featured headline. Calligraphic alphabets serve as a good alternative for traditional Old English. A calligraphic alphabet may be used in all caps, whereas Old English becomes practically unreadable in capital letters only.

ABCDE
FGHIJ
KLMN
OPQRS
TUVW
XYZ
1 2 3 4 5
6 7 8 9 0

CONGO

Legibility plus visual impact are pleasingly integrated in the bold poster alphabet shown here. Congo is an extended alphabet that requires lots of elbowroom on a layout—be it the headline on a poster, truck lettering, window sign, or exhibit panel. The outstanding design characteristic of this unique alphabet is the one-sided serif confined to the upper left of many of the letters. The serif, where it appears, blends gracefully into the basic stroke. Whereas Congo is especially suited where strong visual impact is essential, it lends itself admirably for originally designed letterheads, business cards, and other business forms, especially when the emphasis is on masculinity, strength, and power.

ABCDEFGH
IJKLMNO
PQRSTUVW
XYZ 123456789

CONTINENTAL

A variation of News Gothic (not often associated with newspaper headines), Continental offers its own distinct quality—a highly condensed structure. The hand-lettered alphabet's inside areas or counters, to use the proper typographic term, are extremely narrow. The areas hardly are more than slivers of white space in some cases. Absence of round elements with one exception is another major characteristic this style shares with News Gothic. The exception is the gas pipe-elbow curve serving as a transitional-shape between the main vertical and horizontal strokes. As a highly legible lettering style, Continental is especially appropriate for posters and display work. Current practice is to place letters very close together that compose words, with only a minimum spacing between each letter. One achieves reading rather than each individual letter. Exercise restraint by limiting the use of Continental to one-line copy, or only two lines at the most. Too many words—especially in more than a one-line layout—can result in an astigmatism that affects message legibility and can be disturbing visually because of Continental's highly condensed structure.

ABCDE
FGHIJK
LMNOP
QRSTU
VWXYZ

COOPER

This is a hand-lettered version of the Cooper Display type face which was at the height of its popularity some 30 years ago and, like Broadway, has made a strong come-back in contemporary typography. It is an ideal showcard writers' lettering style. With a fully charged brush, this alphabet can be rendered freehand with a fair degree of speed. You will note a slight fleshy bend in the construction of the serifs and the almost complete absence of straight structural elements, especially conspicuous in the thin strokes. All elements flow into each other casually producing well modulated letter forms. Another marked characteristic of Cooper is the tipped O and Q. The weight of the letters can be modified, depending upon the size of the brush used and the amount of paint carried. For a more casual treatment of this style, try a round-nibbed lettering pen of the Speedball type.

ABCDEFG
HiJKLMN
OPQRSTU
VWXYZ

1234567890

DAMASCUS

Here is a single-stroke lettering style which offers interesting possibilities for practically any type of poster, window display, over-the-door sign, or truck lettering job. It is essentially a one-thickness alphabet with sufficient modification from the basic Gothic to make it "different" and outstanding. The odd-shaped curves give this alphabet a somewhat mid-eastern flavor and create an individuality to make the presentation a welcome departure from the traditional family of Gothic alphabets, long a favorite with sign and bulletin artists. Damascus will add variety to your work. With its mid-east influence, the spacing between letters, as exemplified above, is typical, but the characters can be much more closely spaced, depending on the flavor of the particular application.

ABCDE
FGHIJK
LMNOP
QRSTU
VWXYZ
1234567890

DIGITAL

This rather odd looking alphabet, which
dramatically reflects the computer age we're
living in, is now an accepted member of the
typographic family of alphabets in current
use. It is seen in advertisements dealing
with banking and finance, office machines,
engineering, modern packaging, and archi-
tecture and a host of scientific products
and services. There are countless variations
to the alphabet. The one shown here can
serve as a basic sample which can be modified
by the artist with very little risk of going
wrong. What should be borne in mind,
however, is to retain a measure of consistency
throughout all letters and numbers. Generally
speaking, there is no basic lower case, but
that doesn't mean that one can't be designed,
if it can be made to retain the same
identifying characteristics as the capitals.
You may not use Digital much—but when you
need a sample of the complete alphabet,
you'll be glad you have something to go by
for reference.

ABCDE

FGHIJK

LMNOP

QRSTU

VWXYZ.

DIMENSIONAL

"Today's Super Special;" "Fire Sale;" "Bingo Tonight" . . . All three sign examples are logical applications of the bouncy alphabet featured here. Dimensional is a lot easier to render than it might appear at first glance. Basically, a heavy-set, sans-serif Roman, Dimensional's unique effect is attained by: (a) The drop shadow that falls to the left and lower side of the letter; (b) The topsy-turvy overlapping letters arrangement. For a more conservative effect, the letters in a word need not be off balance. Nor do they have to overlap to achieve the required effect (as indicated in the treatment of the headline above. Either way, the letters may be rendered in outline form, as shown, or the letters can be filled in solidly with a red or other bright color. Special note: It's considerably easier and so much faster to render Dimensional in large, jumbo format rather than in diminutive sizes. First of all, layout the entire word in charcoal or pencil. Then paint in the basic letter forms. Last of all, add the shadows.

A B C D E F
G H I J K L M
N O P Q R S T
U V W X Y Z

a b c d e f g h i j
k l m n o p q r s
t u v w x y z

𝔇iploma

Here is another good alternative lettering
style to Old English. Diploma can be rendered
faster than Old English and is generally more
legible, but it too requires the use of upper
and lower case for ease of legibility. The
Diploma alphabet is closely related to the reed
writing of antiquity and is executed with
either a brush or a broad nibbed pen. It may
be made single-stroke technique or as a built
up letter. If the single-stroke brush technique
is used, pallette the brush well to get a flat
chisel end. To get a natural modulation of
line from a hairline to a heavy stroke, don't
twirl the brush between the fingers—even
around curves. For the hairlines use the side
of the chisel in the same manner as you
would use the side of a flat-nibbed pen. This
lettering style, whether rendered with pen
or brush, is suitable for diplomas, charts,
religious documents, greeting cards, etc. This,
as well as other calligraphic or text alphabets,
allows considerable freedom and latitude
for personal modification. After a little
practice, the natural turn of the lettering tool
will help shape the letters.

ABCDE
FGHIJ
KLMN
OPQR
STUV
WXYZ
1234567890

ELDORADO

As a strongly structured legible letter form,
Eldorado is easily applicable for many
advertising and point-of-sale promotion
assignments. It is especially practical for
posters and window displays. The style lends
itself, too, to three-dimensional cut-out
format for work on exhibit panels that will be
used in industrial shows and the like. A chief
identifying characteristic of Eldorado is its
geometrically circular counters (inside elements) typical of the A, B, and P. Another
characteristic is the rather wide proportion of
each letter form that lends a sense of stability
and stamina to this unusual style. In use,
the alphabet conveys a boldness and a contemporary feel. In execution, snug the letters
up close to each other for most effective
presentation.

ABCDEFG
HIJKLMN
OPQRSTU
VWXYZ
1234567890

ELITE

When next you require a modern alphabet to
endow your layout with an air of formal
elegance and sophistication, Elite should serve
as an excellent model to go by. It is for the
most part a compass and ruling pen lettering
style, takes considerable time to render and
therefore should be reserved mostly for work
intended for reproduction. It is not im-
possible, however, to render it freehand in a
more relaxed technique for showcards for
cosmetic products, haberdashery items, gift
wares, luxury items, etc. For such purposes the
effect of elegance can be achieved without
technical perfection. A watercolor brush
may thus be employed or a lettering pen.
For reproduction purposes (either for screen
printing or other means of producing multiple
copies), mechanical instruments are required
for precision and accuracy if one is to do
justice to this modern alphabet style.

ABCDEFG
HIJKLM
NOPQRS
TUVWX
YZ
1234567890

ESQUIRE

Here is a unique alphabet, highly distinguish-
able by its flattened top and bottom elements which ride flush with the upper and
lower guidelines. Other distinguishing
characteristics are the slightly triangularized
lobes that are evident in the letters, B, D, O, P,
etc.; the unusual upturns on some of the
serifs, the contoured strokes of many of the
letters, and the curvular crossbars of the
A, E, F, and H. Though Esquire suggests a
slightly archaic appearance, it is an alphabet
which fits in unhesitatingly with modern
typography vogue. It affords a great range
of applications to many advertising media—
showcards, truck lettering, store displays,
television titles, bookjackets, as well as for
general newspaper advertisements. With
experience, Esquire can be rendered with equal
ease as a freehand lettering style with
lettering brush or steel pen.

ABCDEF
GHIJKL
MNOPQ
RSTUV
WXYZ
1234567890

FLORIDIAN

Essentially Floridian is a single-thick, one stroke alphabet which looks ornate and "fancy free" but is easy to render and permits countless variations in flourishes and swash ornamentation. It may be used for initials as well as for complete words if the copy is limited, and it acts as an excellent contrast or foil for more basic and traditional alphabets employed in combination on the same job. Here is a free-flowing fast lettering style that lends itself equally well to brush or pen. The predominance of flourishes suggests its use for products and services of primary appeal to women buyers, but this alphabet is by no means so limited in scope. Floridian is an appropriate alphabet for one word captions and short headlines for posters, paper signs, and displays dealing with flowers, cosmetics, travel, silverware, furs, art and gallery exhibits, and the like.

ABCDE
FGHIJ
KLMNO
PQRS
TUVW
XYZ
1234567890

FRISCO

The wrought-iron filigree effect of Frisco is achieved by the thickness of the strokes that softly blend into one another with the serifs which are bracketed mostly into the basic strokes. Note the unusual construction of the J, L, and P; the center elements inside the open area of the O and the Q; and the disconnected cross strokes of the A, B, H, and R. Frisco is essentially a freehand lettering style where absolute precision of construction is not only unnecessary but is not typographically desirable. The basic strokes are slightly curved—thus eliminating the use of a ruling pen or other mechanical instrument. If three-dimensional lettering is called for, Frisco is in good taste as a choice for cut-out work on wood, display board, metal, or other kinds of rigid material. The letters in the Frisco alphabet will hold up well because not any vulnerable construction elements are there to worry about.

ABCEE
GHIJK
LMNOP
QRSTU
VWXYZ

FRONTIER

Bold, big, and blustering—these aptly
describe this alphabet, typical of the character of the Western plains and the men who
opened our frontiers beyond the Mississippi.
The heavy block-like serifs are among the
common marks of identification of the
Barnum alphabets series of which this is a
member. An added point of identification,
quite distinct in itself, is the curved stems
which blend into the serifs. Frontier is an
excellent display letter which will add stamina
to any headline of a layout. As such the
alphabet offers possibilities for application
to many commercial uses—posters, truck
lettering, exhibition panels, titles for trade
journals, and the like. Because of its rugged
construction, this is a good alphabet to consider when designing work to be cut in wood,
metal, and plastics. For best effect, when
laying out the copy, the letters should be close
together, with a minimum of space. Closely
spaced, the finished copy holds together well,
and is seen as complete words or phrases,
rather than isolated letters.

ABCDE
FGHIJK
LMNOP
QRSTU
VWXYZ
1234567890

GOTHAM

SLUG—GOTHAM . . . .
A bold easy-to-read alphabet, Gotham will
be a practical addition to your growing
repertoire of hand-lettered alphabets. It can
be executed in a single stroke technique—
if the brush is heavy enough and well palletted
—or by a more carefully build-up technique.
The technique you decide to use will be
governed largely by the needs of the occasion
and the time you can devote to it. You'll
note the slight curvature in most strokes—
a characteristic which gives this popular
alphabet an informal touch, and at the same
time makes it easier and faster to render.
When your next lettering project calls for
a bold poster treatment, keep Gotham in
mind!

ABCDE
FGHIJK
LMNOP
QRSTU
VWXYZ

GOTHIC DISPLAY

This is a powerful lettering style ideally suited for poster work. The top and bottom of each letter is flattened so that the lettering lies flush with the guide line, as evident in the C, G, J, K, S, etc. Most of the letters seem to fit into—and pretty well occupy—the confines of a square. A line of Gothic Display on a poster appears as a solid block, with the white areas within the letters giving texture to the mass. This lettering style lends itself admirably for screen printing or other forms of graphic reproduction. There are no thin lines to worry about or break whether the letters are printed direct (black on white) or reverse (white on black). In addition, the stocky construction of this letter form makes it a good choice for three-dimensional cut-out lettering in any material—beaver board, wood, metal, plastic, etc. It is a basic style that you'll find most practical.

ABCDEFG
HIJKLMN
OPQRST
UVWXYZ
1 2 3 4 5 6 7 8 9 0

GRAFFITI

The scribble lettering that decorates (and defaces) today's walls, fences, and public building facades through permissiveness has attained the level of a unique contemporary art form. The alphabet shown here—modified for more applicable commercial use— reflects the informality of graffiti writing as well as the more acceptable family of cartoon alphabets that long have been with us. For best results, this type of lettering must be done spontaneously and with "controlled" abandon. Usually the brush is not pivoted but is used front and side of the bristle, as the natural swing of the hand guides it in the formation of the component strokes. Though absolute uniformity is not called for, nor even desired, the essential character and "color" must be retained. The sample illustration certainly is not "basic"—just something to copy. Rather it is a guide to help you in designing your own version of the Graffiti style. A flat chiseled brush or pointed water-color brush will do. Each has its own built-in characteristic in the final effect.

ABCDEF
GHIJKL
MNOPQ
RSTUV
WXYZ
1234567890

GRAFIK

Here's another lettering style that deserves top of the list priority in your growing collection of practical alphabets. It's called Grafik and it possesses typographic qualities, the most outstanding of which is legibility. This makes it an ideal choice for lettering on posters, truck panels, and signs of all kinds. But as broad as this range is, Grafik has practical applications for use in diverse advertising purposes in newspaper and magazine ads, cover designs for annual reports, souvenir journals, menus, and the like. Devoid of time consuming curlicues and other typographic frills, this lettering style can be rendered with comparative dispatch by a competent lettering craftsman, either free hand or with a ruling pen, depending upon the degree of finish required in the final application.

ABCDEFG
HIJKLM
NOPQRS
TUVW
XYZ
1234567890

HARVARD

The distinguishing characteristic of this single-thick alphabet is the conspicuous presence of bold serifs which do not run through the basic strokes (as they do in most conventional serif alphabets) but stop halfway, protruding right and left. Another obvious point of identification is the absence of round elements, except at corner joints, which blend vertical and horizontal strokes. You will note too that there is little variation in the relative width of the letters with the exception of the M and W, which take up more room. Because of the comparative uniformity in width, letter spacing is not much of a problem. As to the practical application of this structurally consistent alphabet—college campus publicity, engineering and building trade advertising, signs and displays for banks and financial institutions suggest themselves first. If you intend to employ this lettering style for screen printing reproduction, you will make a wise choice. For most purposes, the art can be carefully rendered in pencil only, and hand-cut in film without filling in with ink or paint. What's more, the absence of wispy hairlines and thin strokes assures clearly printed results without undue fuss or special "nursing."

ABCDEFG
HIJKLMN
OPQRSTU
VWXYZ
1234567890

HONDA CAPS

This is a hand-drawn version of a powerful poster alphabet produced as a phototype by the Alphatype Corporation of Illinois. Devoid of serifs, the alphabet lends itself admirably to fast brush work using a short-haired chisel lettering brush, well paletted, deftly handled so that each stroke is sharp, definite, and vigorous. It lends itself also to the flat, broad-nibbed pen or felt tipped magic marker, the degree of finish depending upon the nature of the assignment. Because of the broad elements of the basic strokes, a decorative insert, inline, or other embellishment is feasible and highly effective. Somewhat reminiscent of religious overtones, Honda Caps can serve as a simplified variation to Old English. As such it has a double virtue—it is far more legible and very much faster to render than the traditional Old English alphabet styles. Honda Caps is bound to become a favorite with you as it has with so many other lettering artists and designers.

ABCDE
FGHIJK
LMNOP
QRSTU
VWXYZ

ITALIC

Practically any lettering style, properly slanted, becomes italic. The slant must be consistently maintained. If you have difficulty in this respect, draw diagonal guidelines with a pencil, by tipping the paper to the proper angle, taping it to the drawing board, and using the T-square in the usual manner. After a while, you will not have to resort to this, as your eye is trained and you automatically slant the letters in the same direction. Even then, for a careful rendering of any letter form, especially for reproduction, most lettering artists draw in guidelines where precision is a technical requirement. Italics are used for emphasis and for best effect, the lettering must be confined to a word or phrase. Extensive wording in italics is difficult to read and should be avoided. Historically, italic lettering styles were developed and brought to perfection in Italy by early scribes, hence the derivation of the term italic.

ABCDE
FGHIJ
KLMN
OPQR
STUV
WXYZ
1234567890

LATHAM

Latham should be applied where individuality
rather than run-of-the-mill legibility is what
your client is after. As such a style, Latham
has myriad uses. It's suitable as a com-
pany's identification on its labels, letterheads, and so forth. It's not out of place
either in presentation of a briefly worded
message that will appear on posters or similar
displays. Latham is a mechanical instrument-
rendered alphabet, essentially, where traditional letter shapes are reduced to geometric
forms. Compasses and ruling pens are prime
tools in producing Latham. And a small
lettering brush should be on hand for
rendering the transitional curves. With today's
ever-increasing trend toward specially designed alphabets—many not ever really
elevated to the rank of "hot metal" printers'
type faces—a hand-lettered style such as
Latham reflects the individuality and distinction of the current typographic mode.

ABCDEFG
HIJKLMN
OPQRST
UVWXYZ
1234567890

LORELEI

Here is a novel letter form that will lend an
airy, breezy outdoor look to any piece of copy.
Naturally the wording must be consistent
with the frilly spirit of the alphabet. That's
where aesthetics and discretion of the artist
enter into consideration. Evidently Lorelei is
not an all-purpose letter form. It has a
whimsy and gaiety which limits its application
—so be sure to put it in the proper category
in your source file of alphabets. When is
Lorelei a likely candidate for putting it into
practical use? Here is a sampling of suggested uses: Showcards and posters dealing
with flowers and gardening, finely structured
wrought-iron furniture, greetings for festive
occasions, musical recitals, advertising
lettering for posters and window displays for
cosmetics, furs, jewelry, and other finery.

One of the chief identifications of this alphabet is the absence of any straight
mechanically ruled lines and the introduction
of hairspring curlicues.

ABCDE ·
FGHIJK
LMNOP
QRSTU ·
VWXYZ
1234567890

METRO

Metro is based on a currently popular type
face called Microgramma. The alphabet is a
hand-lettered version which introduces a
variation in thickness—a characteristic
of the original type face. Broadly speaking (no pun intended), the letters of this
alphabet are uniformly wide and require
lots of space in the forming of words. It is a
style, therefore, that is suited to one-line copy
mainly, such as advertising headlines, titles
of books, and the like. Metro belongs in the
category of "gas pipe" lettering—that is,
all basic strokes that are conventionally made
round, such as the C, O, Q, are flattened to
vertical uprights as are the lobes of the B, P
and other component elements, which are
generally round. This style is appropriate for
lettering which is to convey a feeling of
strength, security, and mechanical stability.
It's an excellent choice, therefore, for industrial exhibits, banking institutions, posters and
displays dealing with the graphic arts, men's
apparel, engineering, and building projects.
The lettering artist has ample latitude to vary
the width of the letter form to fit space requirements, but must bear in mind that too
much condensation will mar the basic characteristic which identifies this modern alphabet.

ABCDEFG
HIJKLMN
OPQRSTU
VWXYZ
1234567890

MODERN HALF BLOCK

The hand-lettered alphabet shown here is a
modern variation of a traditional sign painter's
alphabet commonly identified as Half Block.
Its renewed popularity today is evidenced
by the fact that it has been recently released
as a photo lettering style intended for use as
headlines for newspaper and magazine
advertising, brochures, and posters. It is also
available in precut form in cardboard, wood,
and plastic in a variety of sizes and thicknesses.
The distinguishing characteristics of this bold
sans-serif alphabet are the obliquely cut
"corners," the complete absence of round
elements and the fairly uniform thickness
throughout. Modern Half Block can best be
rendered as a "one stroke" alphabet by
employing a well paletted chisel—edged brush
or a broad nibbed steel pen matched to
suit the desired thickness of the stroke.

ABCDEFG
HIJKLM
NOPQRS
TUVW
XYZ
1234567890

NEVELE

To the casual eye of the average person, the fine structural differences and nuances between one alphabet and another are hardly discernible. In most cases all alphabets look alike to him until the distinguishing differences between them are pointed out. This is not the case with Nevele, an alphabet possessing unique features. The notable characteristic of this alphabet—namely, the triangular zigzag structural elements—makes the letters easily identifiable and radically "different." Nevele is a good alphabet to have on hand when you need to give the advertiser something that is a real attention getter. Because of its Greek, somewhat cuneiform structure, Nevele is appropriate for work relating to old historic events, classic musical and theatrical programs, art exhibits, biblical themes, and similar events.

ABCDEFG
HIJKLMN
OPQRST
UVWXYZ
1234567890

OPEN FACE ROCKWELL

This alphabet is modelled after Norman Rockwell's lettered signature on his famous magazine covers and illustrations. The recent revival of Rockwell's illustrations makes this alphabet both timely and appropriate. Open Face Rockwell can be rendered in pen or brush with equal ease. For "reproduction-perfection" purposes, a ruling pen can be put to service for most of the basic strokes. A well selected second color placed within the open areas will add appreciably to the general effect, where a decorative quality is desired.

ABCDE
FGHIJ
KLMN
OPQRS
TUVW
XYZ
1234567890

PAPER STENCIL

The Paper Stencil alphabet will surely be one of the most practical alphabets in your repertoire of quick short-order lettering styles for rush jobs. It may be made one-thickness or varied somewhat to take on a thick-and-thin format. Screen printing shops which cater to repeat orders for supermarket window banners will find this alphabet especially practical for cutting paper stencils without the worry and fret that the inside areas of letters such as the A, B, O, P, Q, and R will drop off during the adhesion or while the printing is in progress. The little ties keep the stencil sheet intact securely and for short or long runs. For brush lettering purpose, the alphabet can be rendered with as heavy a brush as you can manage, or if you have become adept working with felt tip-markers, you will manage to get additional character into the alphabet by the shape and width of the marker.

ABCDE
FGHIJ
KLMN
OPQR
STUV
WXYZ
12345
67890

PiNTO

A modification of the gothic one-thickness
letter form, Pinto is unique in the cut-away
structure evident in many of the letters of the
alphabet. It has a strong graphic quality
which makes it a good choice for contemporary advertising in any form—posters,
banners, displays, TV commercials, etc.
It is an easy letter form to render with brush,
and an extra-wide felt marker for general
jobs. For more precise rendering, as for reproduction purposes, it may be rendered with
ruling pen and straight-edge. The corners
can be rounded, as shown, or made square.
The proportion can be varied; it can be
extended in width for added stamina. Pinto
will be a welcome addition to the repertoire
of practical alphabets specially suitable for
screen printing reproduction. Not only will
it print well (direct or reverse), but the stencil
can be cut easily and quickly in paper or film.
It is essentially a display letter meant for
feature copy and headlines.

ABCDEFG
HIJKLMN
OPQRST
UVWXYZ
1234567890

POSTER GOTHIC

Poster Gothic is a hand-lettered version of a standard type face of the same name. Basically a sans serif letter with slight variation between thick and thin stroke, the alphabet is a natural for themes suggestive of mystery, intrigue, power, and brute masculinity. Well rendered, Poster Gothic has a terrific impact on any advertising message—be it on posters, banners, large paper signs, and the like. Needless to say, discretion must be exercised in limiting its use to a headline or, at most, to a line or two of copy. Another good "special purpose" adphabet to add to your growing collection!

ABCDEF
GHIJK
LMNOP
QRSTU
VWXYZ
1234567890

RODEO

This is an original lettering style that you may find useful when you tire of "basic" alphabets and want to give your customer something unique. However, the occasion must call for it, since this alphabet is not strong on legibility. What may such occasions be? Window displays, posters, or paper signs for flowers, jewelry, furs, musical instruments or recitals, and the like. This alphabet lends itself for more masculine applications as well. It was used successfully for a riding academy and horse show promotion and seemed admirably suited for the job on hand. You will find Rodeo a good addition to your stable of "special" alphabets for an active subject or one expressing an air of urgency.

ABCDEF
GHIJKL
MNOPQ
RSTUV
WXYZ
1234567890

ROYAL

Although a slightly ornate alphabet, this
style is simple to construct. With developed
dexterity, Royal can be rendered with ease
and dispatch. Essentially a Roman letter
form, it departs from the conventional format
in curvular strokes of basic elements. Note
the crossbars of the A and H; the tilted
position of the O and Q; the wispy terminals
that serve as serifs. Complete absence of
rigidity or mechanical structure makes Royal a
"natural" to do stencil-cutting for screen
printing. Because of the comparatively stocky
weights of all the letter strokes, furthermore,
the printing results are excellent in a positive
or a negative image. Observe there are no
lines to break or run in. Royal's exceptional
versatility qualifies its use especially on
posters, paper signs, fliers, brochures. The
style adapts well for nearly every purpose,
however, where legibility plus a distinctive
quality are of paramount importance.
You'll be glad to welcome Royal to your
growing collection of practical alphabets.

ABCDEF
GHIJKLM
NOPQR
STUVW
XYZ
1234567890

SARATOGA LIGHT

Here is a simple but versatile showcard lettering style that you will want to add to your growing repertoire of alphabets. Suitable both for pen and brush, Saratoga Light is basically a one-thickness letter with slight variations in thickness that come naturally with variations in pressure of the lettering tool used. Cross bars are below optical center, the B is intentionally top heavy, as also are the P, R, and S, producing an unique effect specially suited for advertising dealing with software, finery, and things feminine. With a little experience, professional speed can be attained so that Saratoga Light can be made use of for fast "knock out" jobs as well as for a more careful treatment when the occasion (and price you get) calls for it.

A B C
D E F G
H I J K
L M N
O P Q R
S T U V
W X Y Z

SENTINEL

Your own handwriting often can serve as an excellent basis for creating an original style alphabet. The alphabet shown here is a modification of handwriting with a free-flowing flourish that can best be achieved with spontaneity. It may be rendered several ways— each with characteristics all its own—with water-color brush, pen, or with fine-pointed felt marker. For added accent in the center of the stroke, this style may be done by a build-up technique; that is, by additional strokes finely blended into the center of the curves. It may be rendered as a one-thickness letter form, retaining the flourish but without the accented weight. Sentinel is a good choice for work reflecting a feminine touch. It can be done with endless modifications depending upon mood and purpose. Aside from its commercial applications, this flourish alphabet in capitals is an excellent choice for personal stationery, embroidery, and engraved initials. Don't attempt to copy this alphabet as you see it here, but rather use it as a guide by which you can create your own.

ABCD
EFGHI
JKLM
NOPQ
RSTU
VWXYZ

SIROCCO

Sirocco is a unique alphabet with strong calligraphic influence, as evidenced in abrupt twists and turns and free-flowing strokes. Somewhat reminiscent of the Orient and Hebrew letter structure, Sirocco is an ideal alphabet to consider when designing a layout with a biblical theme, or the wasteland of the desert and romance. As such it would be an appropriate alphabet for displays and posters featuring exotic perfumes and spices. Although the alphabet illustrated here was rendered with brush, a broad-nibbed pen and oblique tipped felt marker could well be used—each tool of course leaving its own imprint in the final result. The decorative device shown at the upper left side of the "A" could be lengthened or shortened depending upon the spacing and letter combination that comprises the words. The same liberty could be taken with the B, P, R, and T, thus making it feasible to achieve interesting ligature-like spacing. Sirocco (as well as most of the alphabets featured in this book) is meant to motivate original variations and not intended as an inflexible model for slavish copying. At first, if you wish, use the sample alphabet as shown here; then put aside the sample and develop your own version, retaining where possible the original flavor and style of the speimen.

ABCDEFGH
IJKLMNO
PQRSTUV
WXYZ
1234567890.

SKYLIGHT

With the current vogue for unique alphabets
of a psychedelic nature—something which
reflects the emphasis placed on youth culture
—Skylight should prove of professional
interest. It does not rank high in legibility, but
is strong in conveying a total impression of
mass and mysticism. You will no doubt note
what to your trained eye seems to be a lack
of consistency in the structure of the letter
forms. For example, the F is rather traditional,
so are the A, P, V, W, and X. All other letters
are extremely bottom heavy and apparently
out of proportion. But consistency and nor-
malcy are the hallmarks of the "establishment"
and out of step with today's youth and today's
life style. This alphabet has shock value—
and on this element it bases its claim to our
attention. It should find a place in your
reference file for appropriate, occasional use.

ABCDE
FGHIJ
KLMN
OPQR
STUV
WXYZ
1234567890

SOUTH PAW

The brush-lettered alphabet, South Paw, lends itself exceptionally well to those of us in the profession who are left-handed. One such successful south paw letterer is Bob Kuhnz of Fond du Lac, Wis., to whom we are grateful for contributing an alphabet as well-designed as South Paw. It's a quick one-stroke style that can be easily rendered by left-handed letterers, achieving a typographic quality all its own. For best results it's recommended that the brush be fully charged with paint that's somewhat free-flowing in consistency to avoid dry and rough edges. The thickness of the stroke will vary mostly with the natural width of the lettering tool, but to some extent it will be influenced also by the pressure exerted. Note the abrupt change in weight and direction of most round elements. The abrupt change is due to the fact that the brush is not turned or twirled between the fingers. The brush is held with controlled rigidity, somewhat in the manner of a carpenter's layout pencil or broad, square-edged pen. Indeed it would be interesting to experiment with these tools as an alternate to the traditional showcard brush. South Paw by no means is limited to left-handers. It's a beautiful easy-to-read, easy-to-do style for anyone. South Paw should prove a practical alphabet for posters displays, window banners, and paper signs or try the style wherever a casual or informal effect is desired. Close letter-spacing is suggested so copy reads as complete words or phrases.

ABCDEFG
HIJKLMN
OPQRSTU
VWXYZ
1234567890

SPARTAN

Power, stamina, and vigor are the outstanding characteristics of this interesting lettering style. Spartan, an excellent poster lettering choice, is best rendered with either a short-haired flat brush, well-paletted, or with a broad-nibbed steel lettering pen. Particularly notable is the disconnected oblique-ended crossbar feature evident in many of the letters. The A is typical. Note, too, the short obliquely cut serifs rendered in the same thickness as the basic letter strokes. The next time you're searching for a letter style offering a masculine approach that can be used to advertise a product or service, Spartan may be just the thing you could employ.

ABCDE
FGHIJK
LMNOP
QRSTU
VWXYZ
0123456789

SPEED BRUSH

This hand lettered thick and thin version of
Balloon type face is one of the most popular
alphabets in current use. Speed Brush,
shown here, though designed mainly as a
showcard alphabet, is equally useful for headlines of printed advertisements in newspapers,
magazines, and posters where a note of
informality is desired. There are unlimited
modifications to this alphabet—and I am sure
you will add your own "touch" to create
your own version. The letter form is created
by the deft use of the brush, employing the
face as well as the side of the bristles with a
minimum of twirling, somewhat in the manner
of a pencil. Once you have mastered the
technique, you'll have at your disposal one of
the fastest alphabets in your repertoire—
excellent for paper signs, showcards, banners,
and wherever else character is blended with
speed of production.

ABCDEF
GHIJKL
MNOPQ
RSTUVW
XYZ

SUNDIAL

The alphabet shown here is a hand-lettered
modified version of two standard type faces—
Latin and Chisel. The family characteristics
of these two faces are retained primarily
in the wedge-shaped serifs and the relationship
of thick and thin strokes. The cast shadows
do not actually touch the letter forms and
help to convey a three-dimensional quality
to this highly effective alphabet. You will find
Sundial an easy letter to render if you bear
in mind the basic elements of the Roman
family of type faces. This is one of a series of
hand-lettered alphabets which will be helpful
to you for posters, showcards, exhibits,
as well as the wide range of sign painting
assignments that may come your way.

ABCDEFG
hIJKLMNO
PQRSTUV
WXYZ

1234567890

TABERNACLE

This calligraphic hand-lettered alphabet could very well serve as a variant to Old English, and has many features in its favor. It is far more easy to do, devoid as it is of frills and curlicues. Consequently it can be rendered more quickly. It is more legible than Old English and it can be used all in upper case, whereas Old English cannot—at least it should not. There are unlimited possibilities for modifying Tabernacle, which allows for—and indeed—invites experimentation and the "personal touch." Because of its distinct calligraphic structure, this alphabet can be lettered with a broad nibbed "C" type Speedball pen, oblique tipped magic marker or a well palleted short-haired chisel edged showcard brush. As to its commercial applications—because of its ecclesiastical manuscript characteristics, the alphabet is a "natural" for greeting cards, diplomas and certificates, sign posters and displays with a religious or festive motif, antiques, and the like. It is by no means intended that you copy the alphabet slavishly as it is shown here. Instead let the specimen serve as the starting point or basic structure for a calligraphic style you develop on your own!

ABCDEFG
HIJKLMN
OPQRST
UVWXYZ

1234567890

TEMPEST

If you're looking for a free flowing lettering style to balance your inventory of mechanically structured alphabets, Tempest can fit the bill. There are no straight lines that require the use of a ruler. Tempest is definitely a free-hand lettering alphabet which must be rendered with a degree of casualness—almost cartoon or comic book style. There is a slight variation of thickness in the component strokes which will result quite naturally with the free wrist movement and varying pressure of the brush. Tempest can be rendered in the manner of a one stroke alphabet—and with increasing speed, as confidence is built up with practice. Stroke terminals can be oblique as illustrated on the opposite page or square—as you like—but it's good to remember to be consistent once you have made a choice. Modify, experiment, innovate— but at first with this style, as with all others shown in the series, carefully study the sample before you venture too far afield.

ABCDEF
GHIJKL
MNOPQR
STUV
WXYZ
1234567890

TOLEDO

Toledo is essentially an instrument-rendered lettering style requiring the use of a compass and ruling pen. It is an alphabet that must be carefully matched to the occasion for which it is used. As for example, letterhead design and calling cards for an engineering or construction business, certain types of book-jackets, trade mark and the basic lettering components for a corporate image design, perfume, and cosmetic advertising, etc. The letters are geometric shapes coordinated to form stocky units that hold together very well. An excellent type of screen printing (either in positive or negative form), it is also a good choice for three dimensional cut-out lettering intended for mounting on a backboard panel.

ABCD
EFGHI
JKLM
NOPQ
RSTUV
WXYZ

TORME

A heavy structured alphabet, Torme is a
single-thick block letter. The outstanding
characteristic in the sliver-thin element which
separates the strokes. This feature can
become a deterrent when this style is largely
reduced, which proportionally cuts down on
the sliver, thus running the risk of closing in,
if it is reproduced by screen printing or other
graphic art medium. Torme is strictly an
effect lettering style, and as such, it can be
very appropriate for masculine and industrial
themes on signs and truck lettering. Because
of its stolidness in construction, the alphabet
holds up well for three-dimensional work on
wood, metal, and plastic. There are no serifs
to worry about and no frail elements to break
off in handling. Also, because of its square
base, the letters will support themselves in an
upright position on a base-like or platform-
type construction. For embellishment, color
can be introduced as inlines within each letter
form.

ABCDE
FGHIJK
LMNOP
QRSTU
VWXYZ

TYPO

Typo alphabet is a hand-lettered version of
Typewriter type face, a standard printers'
font very popular for advertising matter
relating to secretarial work, school and office
supplies, editorial copy, and the like.
Essentially a one-thickness letter form, the
chief characteristics of Typo are the elongated
serifs which, as you will note, have a slight
curvature. A flooded showcard brush, fully
charged with paint will yield the proper flow;
however, a similar effect can be achieved
with a large round-headed reservoir pen.
Either way, the results will be effective
and speedy.

ABCDE
FGHIJ
KLMN
OPQRS
TUVW
XYZ

VALENCIA

Valencia is a "special occasion" letter form
that will add variety to your repertoire of hand
lettered alphabets. Discretion will dictate
where this ornate alphabet will be compatible
with the occasion. Though ornate in appearance, Valencia is not inordinately time
consuming to render since there are no
conventional serifs to worry about. Because
of its playful contours and absence of rigid
lines, the natural twist and turn of the brush
(in the hand of a capable craftsman) will
yield the desired results—even when rendered
in a one-stroke technique. An amply sized
chisel is recommended, well-paletted to a fine
edge. Valencia looks good in any size from
greeting card to billboard proportions.
It should be used sparingly either for headlines,
only, or for not more than two or three lines
of copy at most. When that special occasion
arises, Valencia will work for you to your
complete aesthetic satisfaction.

ABCDEF
GHIJKL
MNOPQR
STUV
WXYZ
1234567890

YORK

York, the sans-serif alphabet, is a derivative of a standard type face known as Broadway, a type design which has enjoyed continued popularity through the years. York is characterized by sharp contrasts between the thin and thick elements. The round elements of letters such as C, O, Q are rendered with ink compass to assure mechanical perfection. Similarly, all vertical and diagonal letter components are produced with ruling pen to achieve the mechanical accuracy which gives this alphabet its crisp, clean look. Although based on a traditional type face, York is ultra modern and very much at home on any piece of advertising—be it posters, bookjackets, newspaper and magazine ads, or letterheads. If intended for reproduction, it is well to bear in mind that the thin elements will be in danger of closing in and disappearing if produced in reverse, especially when the letters are greatly reduced in size. To counteract this, it's best to make the thin element somewhat heavier.

A B C D E F
G H I J K L
M N O P Q
R S T U V
W X Y Z

a b c d e f g h i
j k l m n o p q r
s ſ t u v w x y z

𝔉𝔯𝔞𝔨𝔱𝔲𝔯 GERMAN

An alphabet, similar at first glance to the traditional Old English type faces, for years was in traditional use in most newspapers, books, and other printed matter in Germany and Austria. It is still in vogue, currently, though not quite as exclusively as heretofore. There are many variations of this Old German alphabet—as there are many variations of what we call Old English. The sample shown here is known as Fraktur. It is a standard type face with unmistakable calligraphic structure. This is evidenced in the contrasting variation between thick-and-thin strokes and the rather abrupt curves and twists that are the marks of a flat-chiseled, well-palleted brush or pen. In the formation of words, the lower case is always used in conjunction with the capital letters, as is the case with most Old German alphabets. There is a far greater frequency in employing capitals as the initial letter of words, because in the grammar of the German language, all nouns are spelled with an initial capital letter preceding the lower case letters. Note the wide disparity in the structure between upper and lower case letters—another unique characteristic of Fraktur. There is an additional letter in the lower case alphabet—making it a 27-letter alphabet. In the lower case you'll note the letter "s" is followed by one quite different as a word's last letter.

ΑΒΓΔΕ
ΖΗΘΙΚ
ΛΜΝΞ
ΟΠΡΣ
ΤΥΦΧ
ΨΩ

ΕΛΛΑΣ GREEK

The 24-letter Greek alphabet is basically the
same as it was in Athens way back in the
5th Century B.C. It is interesting to note that
many of the letters were taken over later
by the Romans and have been integrated
into our own alphabet—the common alphabet
used in the U.S., Great Britain, Spain, France,
and many other countries. History relates
that the Greeks adopted 16 letters from the
early Phoenician traders who in turn are said
to have gotten them from the Egyptians.
It is from the Greeks that we derive the word
"alphabet." The word consists of a combination of the first two letters of the alphabet
Alpha (A) and Beta (B). The Egyptians are
generally credited with the development of
language in the written form, having more than
5,000 years ago devised a workable form of
written communication in the form of picture
writing or hieroglyphics. The capital letters
of the Greek alphabet are illustrated here.
In most cases, capitals are used exclusively
for advertising purposes. There is a lower
case also which varies considerably from the
basic structure of the capital letters. The
numerals are the same as in ours. Although
there are about 50 different foreign language
alphabets in use today, most of them are
specifically one-language alphabets, such as
Greek, Russian, and Japanese.

אבגדהחוז

חטיכלם

נסעפצק

רשׁת

בכדסוףפץשׁת

עברית HEBREW

The alphabet depicted is the standard Hebrew used in holy scripts—in most Hebrew prayer books. Countless typographic variations are in use today for commercial purposes; for titles of biblical works; for general advertising purposes. The standard type, illustrated here, is a thick-and-thin letter structure, highly calligraphic in quality and effect. It usually is achieved in one stroke, varying the pressure of the pen, brush or whatever other tool may be used. The basic alphabet consists of 21 letters. The bottom two lines of lettering in this alphabet represent auxiliary letters which differ mostly in the placement of a dot which changes the pronunciation and meaning of the finished word. As is well-known, Hebrew is lettered from right to left. It's read the same way. Occasionally there may be a need for reference to the Hebrew alphabet. If you, yourself, do not know the Hebrew language, ask your prospective client to roughly indicate the particular letters that comprise the words of the copy. By using the specimen here you should be able to get by without difficulty.

АБВГДЕ
ЖЗИКЛМ
НОПРС
ТУФХЦ
ЧШЩЪЫ
ЬЭЯЁЙ

РУ́ССКИЙ RUSSIAN

The Russian alphabet, historically referred to as Cyrillian, is based on the characters devised by the 9th Century monk, St. Cyril. It originally consisted of 43 letters, the majority of which closely resembled the Greek alphabet. It is said "an alphabet follows religion." The Cyrillian alphabet was adopted as the national script of all Slavonic people who traced their religion to the Byzantium—the Greek Orthodox faith. The people included in the main the Bulgarians, Serbians, Russians, and the Ukrainians. The Russian alphabet, as it is today, contains a number of letters identical with our own standard Roman alphabet as well as with the formal Greek alphabet. The alphabet is based on the thick-and-thin letter formation, although, of course, it can be modified in a great variety of typographic styles—single thick, with or without serifs, extended, condensed, etc. There is a cursive (hand-written script) and a lower-case alphabet which closely resemble the capital letters. The numerals are the same as ours.